Level **A**

VOCABULARY CONNECTIONS

A Content Area Approach

Program Consultant

Eldon Andersen
First-Grade Teacher
Chula Vista School District
Chula Vista, California

STECK-VAUGHN
ELEMENTARY · SECONDARY · ADULT · LIBRARY

A Harcourt Company

www.steck-vaughn.com

Executive Editor: Diane Sharpe
Project Editor: Amanda Johnson Sperry
Assistant Art Director: Richard Balsam
Design Manager: Jim Cauthron
Photo Editor: Margie Foster
Electronic Production: Tracor Publications

ILLUSTRATIONS

Cover: David Griffin
Content Area Logos: Skip Sorvino

Holly Cooper 34–39, 41, 75–77, 84–85, 87, 90–92, 94, 102–109; Julie Durrell 8–11, 16–17, 19, 22–24, 26, 56–60, 65, 68–70, 72; Michael Krone 30; Dana Regan 52–53, 55.

PHOTOGRAPHY

p. 5 Esbin-Anderson/The Image Works; pp. 6, 7 Grant Heilman/Grant Heilman Photography; p. 20 Alan Pitcairn/Grant Heilman Photography; p. 21 Grant Heilman/Grant Heilman Photography; p. 27 Superstock; pp. 28, 29, 31, 33 Ronald Cohn/Gorilla Foundation; p. 49 Runk/Schoenberger/Grant Heilman Photography; p. 50 A. W. Ambler/Photo Researchers; p. 51 Stephen J. Krasemann/Photo Researchers; p. 66 C. Fournier/The Image Works; p. 67 Lawrence Migdale/Stock Boston; p. 73 Bob Daemmrich/Stock Boston; p. 74 Superstock; p. 75 Nancy Sefton/Photo Researchers; p. 88 W. Cody/Westlight; p. 89 David Young-Wolff/Photo Researchers

ACKNOWLEDGMENTS

Thomas Nelson & Sons, Ltd.: "The Surprise Party" from *Away Went the Hat and Other Stories* by Mary Cockett. Copyright © 1989 by Thomas Nelson & Sons, Ltd. Reprinted by permission of the author.
Penguin Books USA Inc.: "Lunch" from *Digby and Kate* by Barbara Baker, illustrated by Marsha Winborn. Copyright © 1988 by Barbara Baker, text. Copyright © 1988 by Marsha Winborn, illustrations. Used by permission of Dutton Children's Books, a division of Penguin Books USA Inc. "Uncle Foster's Garden Hat," from *Uncle Foster's Hat Tree* by Doug Cushman. Copyright © 1988 by Doug Cushman. Used by permission of Dutton Children's Books, a division of Penguin Books USA Inc.
Random House, Inc.: *Five Silly Fishermen* by Roberta Edwards. Copyright © 1989 by Random House, Inc. Reprinted by permission of Random House, Inc.

ISBN 0-8172-6350-0

11 12 13 14 15 DBH 05 04 03

TABLE OF CONTENTS

Content Area Symbols

 Science   Literature    Social Studies

UNIT 1 FOOD FUN   5

LESSON 1   Eat Your Vegetables!.....................6
LESSON 2 Lunch 12
LESSON 3 From the Tree to You.................20

UNIT 2 SPECIAL FRIENDS   27

LESSON 4 Koko's Friend 28
LESSON 5 The Surprise Party 34
LESSON 6 Thankful for a Friend...............42

UNIT 3 COUNT ON IT   49

LESSON 7   Birthdays for a Tree....................50
LESSON 8   Five Silly Fishermen 56
LESSON 9   It's Time For Kwanzaa!...............66

TABLE OF CONTENTS

UNIT 4   SHARING   **73**

LESSON 10   Sharing Under the Sea 74

LESSON 11   Uncle Foster's Garden Hat........80

LESSON 12   Sharing a Park..............................88

Unit 1 Review 95

Unit 2 Review 96

Unit 3 Review 97

Unit 4 Review 98

Review and Write 99

My Word List...100

Dictionary 102

Answer Key 111

FOOD FUN

We need food. It makes us grow strong and tall. Food can be fun, too. Many people like to grow food. Others like to cook it. And everyone likes to eat food!

In Lessons 1–3, you will read about food. Everyone has favorite foods. What foods do you like best? Write your words on the lines below.

My Favorite Foods

_____

_____

_____

_____

★ Read the story below. Think about the meanings of the words in **dark print**. ★

Eat Your Vegetables!

We eat many different **vegetables**.
This food comes from plants in a garden.
You can buy vegetables at a food **store**.

A carrot is a vegetable.
We do not eat all of the carrot plant.
We eat the **root**.
In a garden, you cannot see the root.
It grows down in the dirt.

Many people love the potato.
It is their favorite vegetable.
Did you know potatoes are not roots?
They are stems of the plant.

We eat the **leaves** of some plants.
You can see these flat, green parts in a garden.
The leaves are **above** the roots.
We eat the leaves of the lettuce plant.

Peas are vegetables, too.
We do not eat all of the pea plant.
We eat the seeds.

Some **flowers** are pretty to look at.
Some smell nice.
All flowers make seeds.
Did you know we eat flowers?
The top parts of broccoli are flowers!

Have fun eating your vegetables!

★ What do the words in **dark print** mean? Other words
  in the story can help you. Draw a line under the words
  that help you. ★

WORD MEANINGS

Read the words in the box. Then write the word for each meaning.

vegetables	root	above
leaves	store	flowers

1. the flat, green parts
of a plant

_____

2. higher than

_____

3. the plant parts that
make seeds

_____

4. a place that sells
things

_____

5. the plant part that
grows in dirt

_____

6. kinds of plants
that we eat parts of

_____

WORD GROUPS

Read the words in the box. Then read each pair of words. Think about how the two words are alike. Write the word from the box that belongs with them.

vegetables	above	root
store		

1. under   on   _____

2. stem   leaf   _____

3. meat   fruit   _____

4. house   school   _____

GET WISE TO TESTS

Which word tells what the picture shows?
Darken the circle for the correct word.

 **Tip** Read each word carefully. Look for the one that tells what the picture shows.

1. ○ wings
   ○ eyes
   ○ lions
   ○ leaves

4. ○ very
   ○ breakfast
   ○ milk
   ○ vegetables

2. ○ above
   ○ in
   ○ about
   ○ beside

5. ○ green
   ○ root
   ○ rabbit
   ○ tree

3. ○ park
   ○ street
   ○ store
   ○ zoo

6. ○ flowers
   ○ seeds
   ○ frogs
   ○ windows

Writing

Many people grow vegetables in a garden. Which vegetables would you plant in a garden? Draw a picture to show your garden. Then tell what your picture shows. Use some vocabulary words.

_____

_____

_____

Turn to "My Word List" on page 100. Write some words you would like to know more about. Choose words from the story or other words. Use a dictionary to find the meanings.

★ Read the story below. Think about the meanings of the words in **dark print**. ★

Lunch

"Something smells good," said Kate.

"I am making **soup** for lunch," said Digby. "Vegetable soup."

"I love vegetable soup," said Kate.
"When will lunch be ready?"

"Soon," said Digby.
"Will you set the table, Kate?
I must **stir** the soup."

Kate set the table.
Digby stirred the soup.
Round and round. Round and round.

**From Digby and Kate,
by Barbara Baker**

"Now will you pour the milk?" said Digby.
Kate poured the milk.
She did not spill a drop.
Digby stirred the soup.
Round and round. Round and round.

"Now we need sandwiches," said Digby.
Kate got cheese and bread.
She made fat cheese sandwiches.
Digby stirred the soup.
Round and round. Round and round.

"How about dessert?" said Digby.
Kate put pudding in glass **dishes**.
She put whipped cream on the pudding.
Digby stirred the soup.
Round and round. Round and round.

"Is the soup ready?" asked Kate.

"Yes," said Digby.
He stopped stirring.

Digby and Kate **ate** vegetable soup
and fat cheese sandwiches.
They ate pudding with whipped cream.
They drank cold milk.
Everything tasted delicious.

Kate looked in the pot.
"There is more soup left," she said.

"Would you like some?" asked Digby.

"No thank you," said Kate.
"I am **quite** full.
You made a wonderful lunch."

"Thank you," said Digby.
"Now it is time to **clean** up, Kate.
Will you wash the dishes?"

"Oh, no," said Kate.
"You can wash the dishes, Digby.
It is *my* turn to stir the soup."

And she did.
Round and round. Round and round.

★ What do the words in **dark print** mean? Other words
in the story can help you. Draw a line under the words
that help you. ★

WORD MEANINGS

Read the words in the box. Then write the word for each meaning.

soup	stir	dishes
quite	ate	clean

1. to wash or make neat

_____

2. things that hold food

_____

3. took in food through
the mouth

_____

4. to mix with a spoon

_____

5. a food made with water
and pieces of other foods

_____

6. very

_____

WORD GROUPS

Read the words in the box. Then look at each pair of pictures. Think about what the pictures show. Write the word from that box that goes with them.

stir	**dishes**	**soup**	**clean**

1.   _____

2.  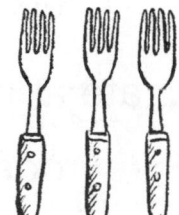 _____

3.   _____

4.  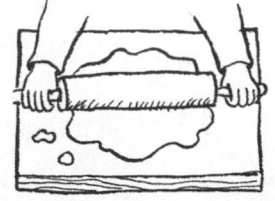 _____

GET WISE TO TESTS

Which answer means the same as the underlined word? Darken the circle for the correct answer.

 **Tip** Use each answer in place of the underlined word. Find the one with the same meaning as the underlined word.

---

1. make <u>soup</u>

- ○ a wish
- ○ a food
- ○ a sound
- ○ a sign

2. <u>clean</u> your ears

- ○ wash
- ○ hold
- ○ cover
- ○ open

3. <u>quite</u> happy

- ○ not
- ○ sometimes
- ○ very
- ○ aren't

4. <u>stir</u> slowly

- ○ grow
- ○ walk
- ○ miss
- ○ mix

5. <u>ate</u> at home

- ○ rode a bike
- ○ took in food
- ○ went to sleep
- ○ sang a song

6. buy new <u>dishes</u>

- ○ plates
- ○ glasses
- ○ clothes
- ○ shoes

Writing

Digby and Kate had vegetable soup and cheese sandwiches for lunch. They had pudding and milk, too. Write some sentences. Tell what you like to eat for lunch. Use some vocabulary words.

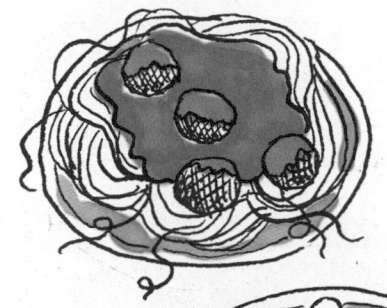

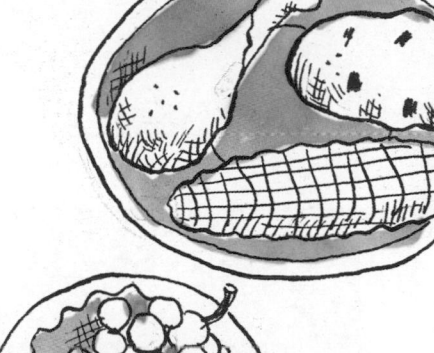

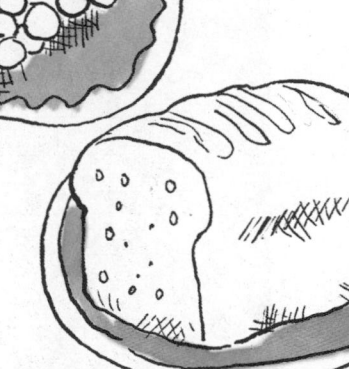

_____

_____

_____

_____

_____

_____

_____

_____

Turn to "My Word List" on page 100. Write some words you would like to know more about. Choose words from the story or other words. Use a dictionary to find the meanings.

★ Read the story below. Think about the meanings of the words in **dark print**. ★

From the Tree to You

Many people eat **oranges**.
This fruit tastes sweet.
It is good for you.
Oranges are grown on farms.
Then they **travel** to you.
Here is how they go from the farm
to your table.

Oranges grow on trees.
The trees need **much** warm sun
to make oranges.
After many days, the oranges are ready.

Workers pick the oranges from the trees.
These people **gather** the fruit by hand.
They put it on big trucks.
The trucks take the oranges to big buildings.

Inside the buildings, the oranges are washed and dried.
A machine then puts them in groups.
Then, the oranges are **packed** into boxes.
Trucks take the boxes to food stores.
At the store, you buy the oranges.
Their trip to you is over!

★ What do the words in **dark print** mean? Other words in the story can help you. Draw a line under the words that help you. ★

21

SENTENCE CLUES

Read the words in the box. Then read the sentences. Complete them with a word from the box.

oranges	travel	much
workers	gather	packed

1. We like to go places. We want to

_____ to the beach.

2. Carlos wants to make juice. He will

buy fresh _____.

3. Mr. and Mrs. Ono were going on a trip. They

_____ some clothes and shoes.

4. There will be a new road in our town. Many

_____ will help build it.

5. The storm did not last very long. We did not

get _____ rain.

6. The squirrel can find food. He will

_____ some nuts.

WORDS WITH THE SAME MEANING

Read the word in dark print. Then read the sentence. Circle the word that has the same meaning as the word in dark print.

1. **packed**   Lisa filled the box with books.

2. **workers**   The helpers leave the job at five o'clock.

3. **gather**   Our class will get cans of food.

WORDS WITH OPPOSITE MEANINGS

Read the word in dark print. Then read the sentence. Circle the word that means the opposite of the word in dark print.

1. **travel**   Next week we will stay home.

2. **much**   We made little money at our cake sale.

PUZZLE FUN

Solve the puzzle. Use the sentences and the words in the box.

oranges	travel	much
workers	gather	packed

Across

1. The _____ get to their jobs early.

2. We will _____ some flowers.

3. Luna _____ her shoes in her bag.

Down

4. They ate apples and _____.

5. My brother didn't have _____ money.

6. You can _____ by boat or car.

Which answer means the same as the underlined word? Darken the circle for the correct answer.

Tip Use each answer in place of the underlined word. Find the one with the same meaning as the underlined word.

1. Please <u>gather</u> the papers.
   ○ burn
   ○ get
   ○ color
   ○ give

2. The <u>workers</u> will fix the window.
   ○ people looking up
   ○ people having fun
   ○ people doing work
   ○ people with books

3. We saw <u>oranges</u> on the trees.
   ○ a kind of fruit
   ○ very small leaves
   ○ drops of rain
   ○ a lot of sun

4. I <u>travel</u> on the bus.
   ○ work
   ○ stand
   ○ see
   ○ go

5. We did not have <u>much</u> paint.
   ○ red and green
   ○ a lot of
   ○ the right
   ○ very pretty

6. Ray <u>packed</u> his lunch.
   ○ didn't like
   ○ threw away
   ○ put together
   ○ laughed at

Writing

People eat oranges in different ways. They cut them in pieces and then eat them. They peel them and eat them. How do you eat an orange? Draw a picture. Then tell what your picture shows. Use some vocabulary words.

Turn to "My Word List" on page 100. Write some words you would like to know more about. Choose words from the story or other words. Use a dictionary to find the meanings.

★ To review the words in Lessons 1–3, turn to page 95. ★

SPECIAL FRIENDS

Friends are special. They play games with you. They laugh with you. Sometimes animals can be good friends, too.

In Lessons 4–6, you will read about some special friends. Think about a friend you have. What do you and your friend like to do? Write your words on the lines below.

Things We Do

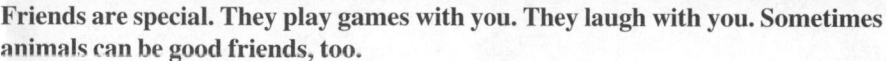

★ Read the story below. Think about the meanings of the words in **dark print**. ★

Koko's Friend

Koko is a gorilla.
Dr. Francine Patterson is a **teacher**.
She showed Koko a way to talk to people.
Koko uses her hands and body
to make words.

Koko wanted a cat. She told Dr. Patterson.
Dr. Patterson found a gray **kitten**.
The little cat had no tail.
Koko **named** him All Ball.

All Ball lived in Dr. Patterson's house.
He went to see Koko every day.
All Ball loved to **visit** his friend.

Koko tried to play games with All Ball.
She **chased** him around the room.
She also liked to tickle the kitten.
But All Ball did not like these games.

All Ball liked to ride on Koko's back.
He loved to be held.
Sometimes All Ball was not very nice.
He would bite Koko.
But Koko was **careful** with All Ball.
She never hurt the kitten.
Koko even painted a picture of All Ball.
Koko loved her little friend.

★ What do the words in **dark print** mean? Other words
  in the story can help you. Draw a line under the words
  that help you. ★

WORD MEANINGS

Write the word for each meaning. Use the words in the box.

visit	kitten	careful
chased	named	teacher

1. a person who shows others how to do something _____

2. gentle _____

3. gave a name to _____

4. a baby cat _____

5. ran after _____

6. to go to see _____

ABC Order

Read each group of words. Then look at the first letter in each word. Write the words in ABC order.

1. a b c d e f

careful _____

flowers _____

above _____

2. i j k l m n

named _____

kitten _____

leaves _____

3. q r s t u v

travel _____

visit _____

quite _____

4. t u v w x y

teacher _____

workers _____

vegetables _____

GET WISE TO TESTS

Which answer means the same as the underlined word? Darken the circle for the correct answer.

 **Tip** More than one answer may make sense. But only one has the same meaning as the underlined word.

1. <u>chased</u> the dog
   - ○ jumped on
   - ○ lived in
   - ○ ran after
   - ○ barked at

2. new <u>teacher</u>
   - ○ fish that bites
   - ○ room at home
   - ○ someone who hides
   - ○ person who teaches

3. white <u>kitten</u>
   - ○ small king
   - ○ baby cat
   - ○ big bird
   - ○ baby duck

4. be <u>careful</u> with
   - ○ sad
   - ○ never
   - ○ gentle
   - ○ away

5. <u>named</u> the baby
   - ○ gave a name to
   - ○ sang to
   - ○ put to bed
   - ○ played with

6. <u>visit</u> a friend
   - ○ wish for
   - ○ go to see
   - ○ need to know
   - ○ smile at

Writing

Koko was a friend to All Ball. She played with him. She was careful with him. How do you show that you are a friend? Draw a picture. Then tell what your picture shows. Use some vocabulary words.

_____

_____

_____

Turn to "My Word List" on page 100. Write some words you would like to know more about. Choose words from the story or other words. Use a dictionary to find the meanings.

★ Read the story below. Think about the meanings of the words in **dark print**. ★

The Surprise Party

Yin-May had spots.
She had spots on her face and
spots on her neck and
spots on her arms.
She had to stay in bed.

"Yin-May called and said she can't come to your **party**," said Mom.

Emma was sad.
"Can I write a **letter** to her?"
asked Emma.
Mom gave her a sheet of paper.

From "**Away Went the Hat**" **and Other Stories,** **by Mary Cockett**

Emma wrote a letter to Yin-May.
This is what Emma wrote.

To
Yin-May

I am sorry you can't come
to my party.

Look out of your window
today at six o'clock.

Have a long piece of string
in your hand.

Love,
Emma

Yin-May read the letter.
"Emma is my **best** friend," she said.
"I **wonder** what the string is for."

"I don't know," said Yin-May's mom.
She found a very long piece
of string for Yin-May.

At six o'clock Yin-May
looked out of her window.
"What a surprise," she said.
She saw all her friends who
had been at Emma's party.
They had balloons and party hats.
They clapped their hands and
waved when they saw
Yin-May at the window.

"Let down the string, Yin-May,"
said Emma.
"But keep one end in your hand."

So Yin-May let down the string and
Emma tied the end to a basket.
Then all her friends put a **present**
for Yin-May in the basket.
There were balloons and candy and
cards and a big piece of birthday
cake from Emma.

"You are a good friend," said Yin-May.
"Now I can join the party, too."

★ What do the words in **dark print** mean? Other words
in the story can help you. Draw a line under the words
that help you. ★

WORD MEANINGS

Write the word for each meaning. Use the words in the box.

party	letter	best
wonder	waved	present

1. a written message   _____

2. better than all others   _____

3. a time for fun   _____

4. moved a hand to say hello
or good-by   _____

5. to want to know   _____

6. a gift   _____

PUZZLE FUN

Solve the puzzle. Use the sentences and the words in the box.

party	letter	best
wonder	waved	present

Across

1. Tia and Beth are _____ friends.

2. Joel saw his aunt. He _____ at her.

3. Mom buys a book. It is a _____ for Juan.

Down

4. Ava got paper. She wrote a _____.

5. I will ask friends to my birthday _____.

6. Chan is late. I _____ where he is.

GET WISE TO TESTS

Which answer means the same as the underlined word? Darken the circle for the correct answer.

Tip Use each answer in place of the underlined word. Find the one with the same meaning as the underlined word.

1. I <u>wonder</u> where he went.
- ○ want to go
- ○ want to stay
- ○ want to know
- ○ want to leave

2. I will send a <u>letter</u> to you.
- ○ surprise
- ○ box
- ○ friend
- ○ message

3. Mother gave me a birthday <u>present</u>.
- ○ card
- ○ gift
- ○ cake
- ○ hat

4. I will wear my <u>best</u> hat.
- ○ bigger than hers
- ○ oldest
- ○ red and white
- ○ better than all others

5. The baby <u>waved</u> at his mother.
- ○ tried to laugh
- ○ made a noise
- ○ moved his hand
- ○ cried a little

6. Tim is having a <u>party</u> at his house.
- ○ pet turtle
- ○ time for fun
- ○ green plant
- ○ big zoo

Writing

Emma was a special friend. Who is your special friend? Why is this friend special? Tell your friend in the letter below. Use some vocabulary words.

Dear _____,

I think you are special because _____

_____

_____

_____.

I am glad we are friends because _____

_____

_____

_____.

Your friend,

_____

Turn to "My Word List" on page 100. Write some words you would like to know more about. Choose words from the story or other words. Use a dictionary to find the meanings.

★ Read the story below. Think about the meanings of the words in **dark print**. ★

Thankful for a Friend

The Pilgrims wanted to pray
in their own way.
They sailed to a land
called America.
It was winter in America.
The Pilgrims did not have much food.
They were cold and **hungry**.

Spring finally came.
It was time to plant seeds.
But the Pilgrims were town people.
They did not know how to grow food.
Squanto was an American Indian.
He was good and **kind**.
He wanted to help the Pilgrims.

Squanto showed the Pilgrims how
to grow beans, **corn**, and other foods.
Squanto told them which plants
in the forest were safe to eat.

The Pilgrims had much food to eat
for the next winter.
They were thankful for the food
and for Squanto.
They asked Squanto to visit.
They **invited** other American Indian
friends, too.
Everyone ate food. They played
games for three days.
It was the **first** Thanksgiving.
Now we have Thanksgiving every year.

★ What do the words in **dark print** mean? Other words
in the story can help you. Draw a line under the words
that help you. ★

SENTENCE CLUES

Read the sentences. Complete them with a word from the box.

kind	hungry	spring
corn	invited	first

1. I like to fly kites. My favorite time of year is

_____.

2. Val planted a garden. She wanted to grow

some _____ to eat.

3. Mr. Perez helped me fix my bicycle. He

is a very _____ man.

4. Gail went to the party early. She wanted to be

the _____ person there.

5. Koji _____ me to play at his

house. He asked Jesse to come, too.

6. I did not eat much lunch. Now it is time for

dinner. I feel very _____.

WORDS WITH OPPOSITE MEANINGS

Read each sentence. Find the word in the box that means the opposite of the underlined word. Write the word on the line.

kind	first	spring

1. _____ My birthday is in the <u>fall</u>.

2. _____ Jose was the <u>last</u> person in line.

3. _____ That bird was <u>mean</u> to the squirrel.

WORD GROUPS

Read each pair of words. Think about how they are alike. Then write the word from the box that belongs with the pair.

invited	spring	corn

1. talked   asked   _____

2. beans   carrots   _____

3. summer   winter   _____

45

ABC ORDER

The words in each group should be in ABC order. Write the missing word. Use the words in the box. The alphabet below can help you.

kind	hungry	spring
corn	invited	first

1. dishes _____ gather

2. present   root   _____

3. invited _____ letter

4. hungry _____ kind

5. _____ dishes   kitten

6. first _____ invited

A B C D E F G H I J K L M N O P Q R S T U V W X Y Z

GET WISE TO TESTS

Which word fits in the blank? Darken the circle for the correct answer.

Tip Read carefully. Use the other words in the sentences to help you choose the correct word.

Hal asked some friends to visit him. He ___(1)___ them to stay for a month. Hal is very ___(2)___ to his friends.

1. ○ left
○ saw
○ invited
○ thanked

2. ○ lost
○ kind
○ angry
○ much

Bill forgot to eat breakfast. He was very ___(3)___. He hurried to be the ___(4)___ person in line for lunch.

3. ○ happy
○ smart
○ brave
○ hungry

4. ○ first
○ last
○ tallest
○ hurt

Ling plants a garden each ___(5)___. This year she wants to grow beans and ___(6)___.

5. ○ day
○ spring
○ winter
○ hour

6. ○ eggs
○ candy
○ corn
○ ham

Writing

The Pilgrims were thankful for Squanto. They were thankful for food, too. Tell some things you are thankful for. Use some vocabulary words.

_____

_____

_____

_____

_____

_____

_____

_____

Turn to "My Word List" on page 100. Write some words you would like to know more about. Choose words from the story or other words. Use a dictionary to find the meanings.

_____

_____

★ To review the words in Lessons 4–6, turn to page 96. ★

COUNT ON IT

How many bugs? How many spots? How many legs? How can you find out? By counting!

In Lessons 7–9, you will read about things people count. We use numbers to count many things. What do you count? Write your words on the lines below.

Things I Count

_____

_____

_____

_____

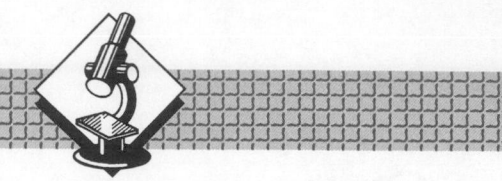

★ Read the story below. Think about the meanings of the words in **dark print**. ★

Birthdays for a Tree

People get older each year.
Trees grow older each year, too.
But how can you find the **age** of a tree?

In a tree, one stem is big and tall.
We call it the **trunk**.
Find a tree that has been cut down.
Look to see where the trunk was cut.
You will **notice** some circles.
These **rings** are bigger at the outside
of the tree.
Each ring shows one year of growing.
Now count the number of rings.

Start with the ring at the very center
of the trunk.
Move toward the **bark** of the tree.
Stop counting at this outside cover.

Some rings are wide.
The tree got much rain and sun in
those years.
The **wood** in the trunk grew bigger
and taller.
Some rings are thin.
The tree didn't get much rain or sun
in those years.

Now you can tell the age of a tree.
Can you find one as old as you?

★ What do the words in **dark print** mean? Other words
in the story can help you. Draw a line under the words
that help you. ★

WORD MEANINGS

Write the word for each meaning. Use the words in the box.

wood	trunk	rings
bark	notice	age

1. the main stem of a tree _____

2. to see _____

3. how old something is _____

4. circles _____

5. the outside cover of a tree _____

6. the inside part of a tree _____

WORDS WITH MORE THAN ONE MEANING

Some words have more than one meaning. Read each sentence. What does the underlined word mean? Circle the picture that shows the meaning.

1. The tree <u>trunk</u> was short.

a.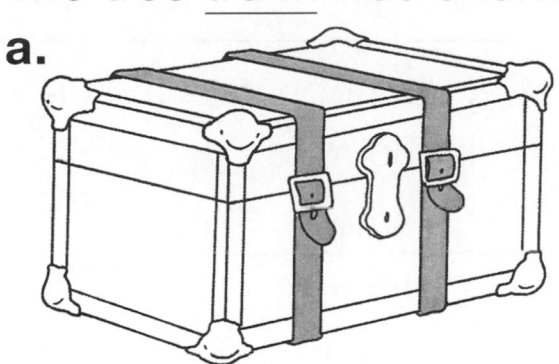
b.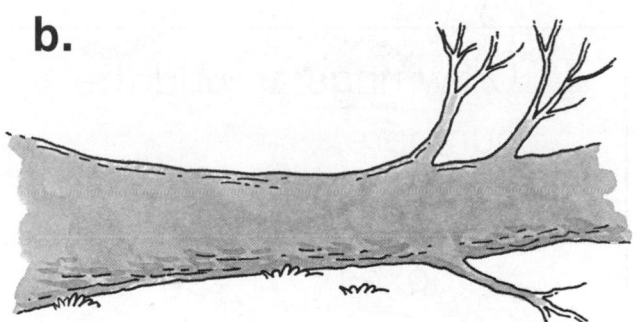

2. Gina <u>rings</u> the bell.

a.
b.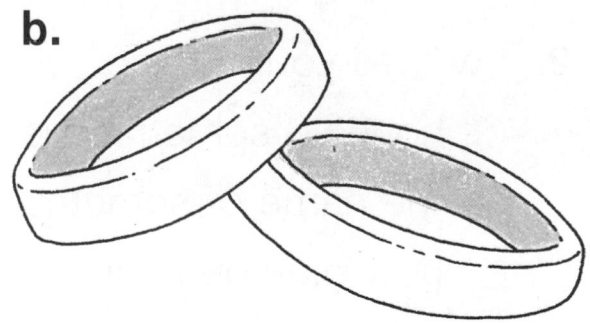

3. The <u>bark</u> helps keep the wood safe.

a.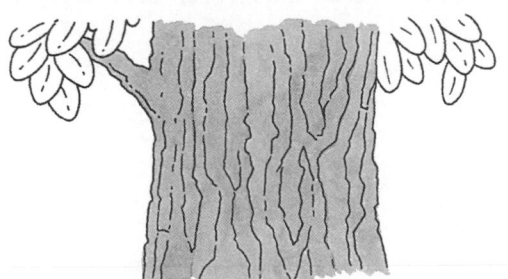
b.

GET WISE TO TESTS

Which answer means the same as the underlined word? Darken the circle for the correct answer.

 **Tip** Use each answer in place of the underlined word. Find the one with the same meaning as the underlined word.

1. Draw <u>rings</u> around the numbers.
- ○ pictures
- ○ boxes
- ○ circles
- ○ stars

2. I will tell you my <u>age</u>.
- ○ how old something is
- ○ the name of something
- ○ how big something is
- ○ where someone lives

3. Our floor is made of <u>wood</u>.
- ○ the leaves of a tree
- ○ the inside of a tree
- ○ the roots of a tree
- ○ the water in a tree

4. I did not <u>notice</u> the car in the road.
- ○ smell
- ○ hear
- ○ want
- ○ see

5. The rabbit ate the <u>bark</u>.
- ○ dog beside a tree
- ○ grass under a tree
- ○ outside cover of a tree
- ○ rings inside a tree

6. Hide behind a tree <u>trunk</u>.
- ○ large leaf
- ○ magic place
- ○ ring inside
- ○ main stem

Writing

How old are you? Draw tree rings to show your age. Use the picture of the trunk below. Then tell what the picture shows. Use some vocabulary words.

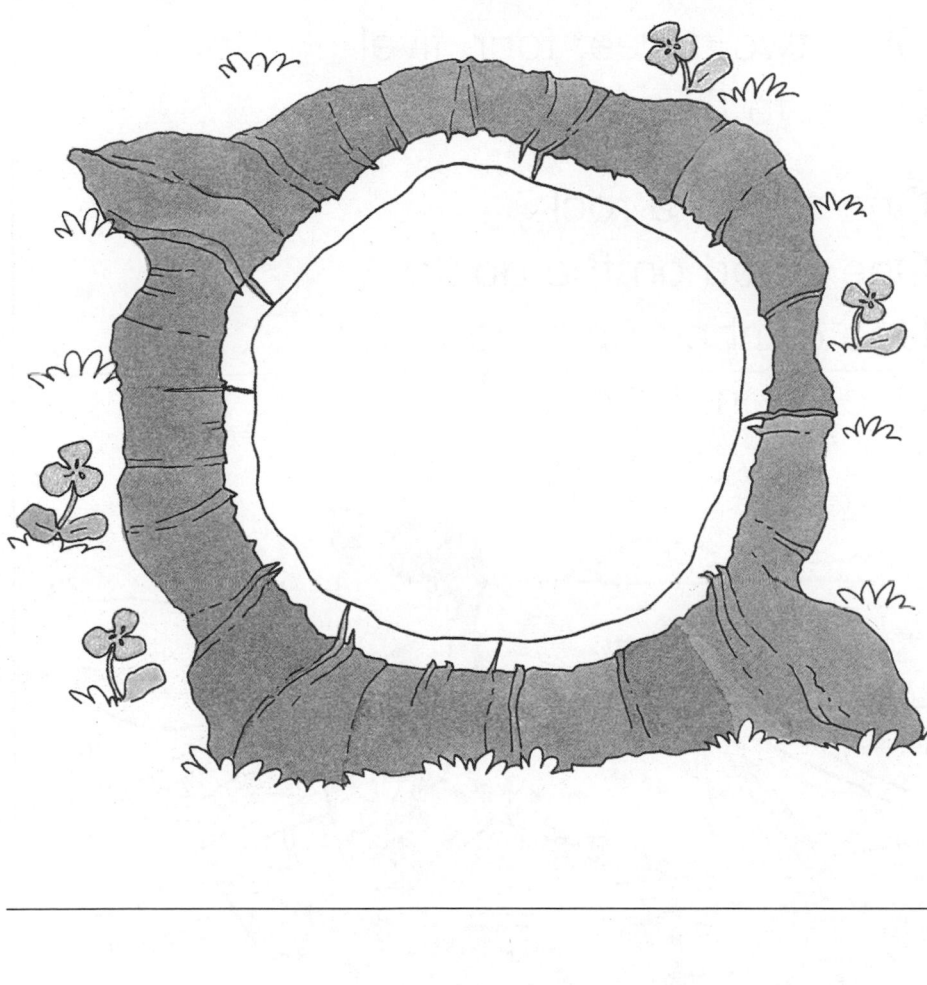

_____

_____

_____

_____

_____

Turn to "My Word List" on page 101. Write some words you would like to know more about. Choose words from the story or other words. Use a dictionary to find the meanings.

★ Read the story below. Think about the meanings of
the words in **dark print**. ★

Five Silly Fishermen

One fine day five fishermen went fishing.
One, two, three, four, five!
Down to the river they ran.

One sat on a rock.
One stood on the dock.
One climbed up a tree.
One lay in the grass.

**From Five Silly
Fishermen, by
Roberta Edwards**

And one fisherman got into a boat.
"Hello, down there!" he called to the fish.
"We are ready to **catch** you!"

At the end of the day each fisherman
had a nice fat fish on his line.
"What a fine **supper** we will have!"
said one fisherman.
"Now let's go home."

"First we must count to see
if we are all here," said another.
"What if one of us fell into the water?"
So he began to count.

"One, two, three, four.
I see four fishermen.
Oh, no! One of us is **missing**!"

"It cannot be!" said another fisherman.
"Maybe you counted **wrong**."
So he began to count.
"One, two, three, four.
I see four fishermen too!
It is true. One of us has drowned!"

All the fishermen hugged each other.
They cried and cried.
"Our poor friend!
What will we do without him?"

Just then a little girl came by.
She was going fishing too.
"Why are you so sad?" she asked them.

"There used to be five of us.
But one drowned," said a fisherman.
"Now there are only four. See!
One, two, three, four," he counted again.

Well, right away the little girl
saw his mistake.
The fisherman **forgot** to count himself.

"Will you give me your fish
if I find your friend?" she asked.

"Yes! Yes!" they said.

"Now jump into the river one at a time,"
the little girl told them.
"And I will count you."

The fishermen did as they were told.
Splash! Into the river they went.
One! Two! Three! Four! Five!

"Five!" the fishermen **shouted**.
"Our lost friend is found!
He did not drown after all!"
The fishermen gave the little girl
all their nice fat fish.

Then home they went.
They were very wet.
They had no fish for supper.
But they were together again!

★ What do the words in **dark print** mean? Other words
in the story can help you. Draw a line under the words
that help you. ★

WORD MEANINGS

Write the word for each meaning. Use the words in the box.

catch	missing	wrong
forgot	supper	shouted

1. lost _____

2. the last meal of the day _____

3. did not remember _____

4. yelled _____

5. not right _____

6. to get _____

WORDS WITH OPPOSITE MEANINGS

Read each sentence. Find the word in the box that means the opposite of the underlined word. Write the word on the line.

catch	missing	wrong
forgot	supper	shouted

1. _____ Taylor <u>whispered</u> my name.

2. _____ Ling <u>remembered</u> to feed her rabbit.

3. _____ Everyone had the <u>right</u> answer.

4. _____ Last night their pet turtle was <u>found</u>.

5. _____ Cruz will <u>throw</u> the green ball.

6. _____ Meg's family had ham for <u>breakfast</u>.

GET WISE TO TESTS

Which answer means the same as the underlined word? Darken the circle for the correct answer.

 **Tip** More than one answer may make sense. But only one has the same meaning as the underlined word.

1. <u>forgot</u> my name
   ○ didn't ask
   ○ didn't remember
   ○ didn't begin
   ○ didn't write

2. the <u>lost</u> watch
   ○ found
   ○ missing
   ○ broken
   ○ newest

3. <u>yelled</u> across the room
   ○ looked
   ○ shouted
   ○ walked
   ○ sang

4. the <u>wrong</u> way
   ○ not far
   ○ not long
   ○ not right
   ○ not sure

5. <u>catch</u> some bugs
   ○ get
   ○ feed
   ○ drop
   ○ need

6. cook <u>supper</u>
   ○ little lunch
   ○ each meal
   ○ much food
   ○ evening meal

Writing

Five Silly Fishermen is a story about fishing. Write your own story about fishing. You can use the pictures to help you. Use some vocabulary words.

_____

_____

_____

_____

_____

_____

_____

_____

_____

_____

Turn to "My Word List" on page 101. Write some words you would like to know more about. Choose words from the story or other words. Use a dictionary to find the meanings.

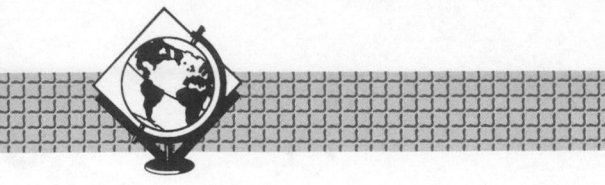

★ Read the story below. Think about the meanings of the words in **dark print**. ★

It's Time For Kwanzaa!

Kwanzaa is a special time for African Americans.
Kwanzaa begins on December 26.
It lasts for seven days.

From the grandfather to the smallest child, the **family** comes together.
They tell things that happened in the past.
They tell the story of people in Africa long **ago**.
They tell the **tale** of African Americans.

Families also tell things they wish for.
Kwanzaa is a time to **hope**.

Candles are an important part of Kwanzaa.
There is one black candle.
There are three red candles and three green candles.
Each candle stands for something special.

Someone lights one candle each night.
Then the person tells about the candle.
The person **explains** what the candle means.

The family has a big party on the last night.
Everyone eats and dances.
They share their feelings about their family and times long ago.

★ What do the words in **dark print** mean? Other words in the story can help you. Draw a line under the words that help you. ★

SENTENCE CLUES

Read the sentences. Complete them with a word from the box.

family	tale	ago
candles	explains	hope

1. It is time for the birthday cake. We need

to light the _____.

2. Tina has many sisters and brothers.

She has a big _____.

3. David and I want to go swimming.

I _____ we can go.

4. It was time for bed. Grandma told us the

_____ of the three pigs.

5. The teacher _____ the

words. Then we understand them.

6. Grandpa was born in 1937. That is a long time

_____.

ABC Order

Read each group of words. Then look at the first letter in each word. Write the words in ABC order.

1. f g h i j k

invited _____

family _____

kind _____

3. r s t u v w

tale _____

shouted _____

wood _____

2. a b c d e f

bark _____

candles _____

ago _____

4. d e f g h i

invited _____

hope _____

explains _____

PUZZLE FUN

Solve the puzzle. Use the sentences and the words in the box.

family	tale	ago
candles	explains	hope

Across

1. Dinosaurs lived long _____.

2. Mom _____ the problem to Dad.

3. Please don't tell a scary _____.

Down

4. There are two boys in my _____.

5. I am very hungry. I _____ we eat soon.

6. It is dark. We will light the _____.

Which word fits in the blank? Darken the circle for the correct answer.

 **Tip** Read carefully. Use the other words in the sentences to help you choose the correct word.

Pepe read a book. It was a ___(1)___ about a fox. The fox lived many years ___(2)___.

1. ○ picture   **2.** ○ now
     ○ tale   ○ tonight
     ○ song   ○ ago
     ○ word   ○ old

It is my birthday. Dad lights the ___(3)___ on my cake. Then everyone in my ___(4)___ sings "Happy Birthday."

3. ○ lamp   **4.** ○ chair
     ○ name   ○ world
     ○ wood   ○ family
     ○ candles   ○ present

We want to go to the park. We ___(5)___ Dad will take us. Dad says no. He ___(6)___ that it might rain.

5. ○ thank   **6.** ○ sits
     ○ make   ○ explains
     ○ hope   ○ asks
     ○ help   ○ sings

Writing

Kwanzaa is a special time. Other days in the year are special, too. What is your favorite special day? What do you like about that day? Draw a picture. Then tell what your picture shows. Use some vocabulary words.

Turn to "My Word List" on page 101. Write some words you would like to know more about. Choose words from the story or other words. Use a dictionary to find the meanings.

★ To review the words in Lessons 7–9, turn to page 97. ★

SHARING

There are many ways to share. You can give something to another person. You can do something for another person. Sharing makes us feel good.

In Lessons 10–12, you will read about sharing. People share. Animals share, too. What things do you share with others? Write your words on the lines below.

Things I Share

_____

_____

_____

_____

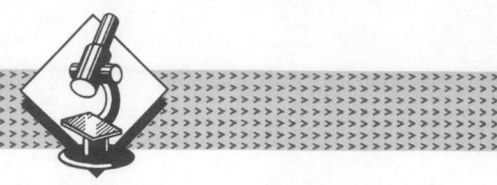

★ Read the story below. Think about the meanings of the words in **dark print**. ★

Sharing Under the Sea

A clown fish is a very small animal.
This **tiny** fish is orange and black
and white.
Its colors make it look like a clown.
The sea anemone looks like a flower.
It is really an animal.

The clown fish lives with the sea anemone.
It is safe there.
Other sea animals cannot get it.
The anemone stings them.
The sting does not hurt the clown fish.
It has a special **coat** that covers its body.

The clown fish helps the anemone get food.
The clown fish **drops** food as it eats.
Other fish try to get the falling food.
They swim **close** to the anemone.
The anemone stings them when
they come near.
Then the anemone eats the fish.

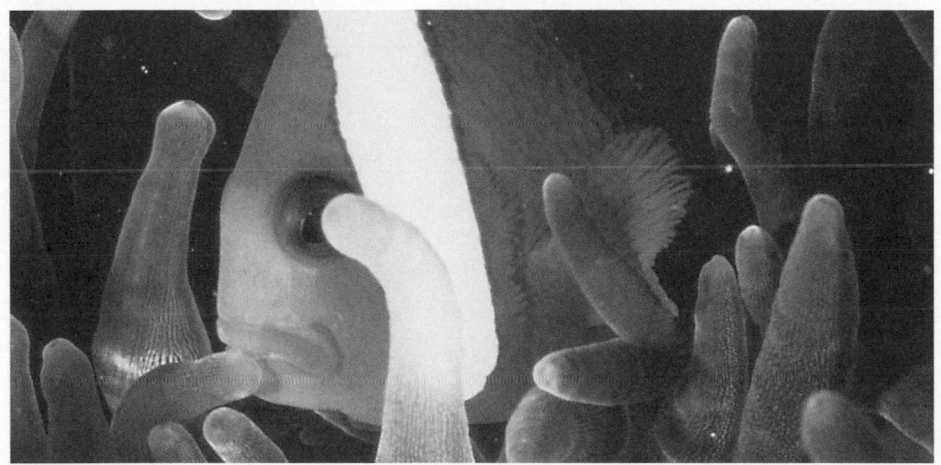

Bits of dirt and food get on the anemone.
The clown fish eats these little pieces.
Plants grow on the clown fish.
The anemone cleans them off.

The sea anemone and the clown fish
take care of each other.
Both are good at sharing.

★ What do the words in **dark print** mean? Other words
in the story can help you. Draw a line under the words
that help you. ★

WORD MEANINGS

Write the word for each meaning. Use the words in the box.

tiny	both	coat
drops	close	bits

1. lets fall _____

2. near _____

3. very little _____

4. small pieces _____

5. something that covers _____

6. the two _____

WORD GROUPS

Read each pair of words. Think about how they are alike. Then write the word from the box that belongs with them.

tiny	both	close

1. all   some   _____

2. little   small   _____

3. here   near   _____

WORDS WITH MORE THAN ONE MEANING

Some words have more than one meaning. Read each sentence. What does the underlined word mean? Circle the picture that shows the meaning.

1. Some animals have a <u>coat</u> of fur.

a.    **b.**

2. We saw <u>drops</u> of water on the window.

a.    **b.**

GET WISE TO TESTS

Which answer means the same as the underlined word? Darken the circle for the correct answer.

 **Tip**   Use each answer in place of the underlined word. Find the one with the same meaning as the underlined word.

1. A <u>tiny</u> mouse was in the shoe.
   - ○ very mean
   - ○ very tall
   - ○ very little
   - ○ very soft

2. We gave my room a <u>coat</u> of paint.
   - ○ covering
   - ○ cleaning
   - ○ warming
   - ○ feeling

3. We ate <u>bits</u> of apple.
   - ○ long lines
   - ○ hard sticks
   - ○ small pieces
   - ○ toy trains

4. The dog <u>drops</u> the ball.
   - ○ barks at
   - ○ lets fall
   - ○ gets stuck
   - ○ runs after

5. The teacher gave books to <u>both</u> of us.
   - ○ all
   - ○ just some
   - ○ the two
   - ○ only one

6. Come <u>close</u> and look at the picture.
   - ○ far
   - ○ there
   - ○ now
   - ○ near

Writing

The clown fish and the anemone live together. What other kinds of animals live together? Draw a picture. Then tell what your picture shows. Use some vocabulary words.

Turn to "My Word List" on page 101. Write some words you would like to know more about. Choose words from the story or other words. Use a dictionary to find the meanings.

★ Read the story below. Think about the meanings of the words in **dark print**. ★

Uncle Foster's Garden Hat

"What is that hat?" Merle asked.

"That is my garden hat,"
Uncle Foster said.

"It is old now.
But I remember
when it was brand–new."

I was out in the garden.
It was very hot.
I took off my hat
and laid it on the **ground**.
Then I went to the shed
for my hoe.

From <u>Uncle Foster's</u>
<u>Hat Tree,</u> by Doug
Cushman.

When I returned, my hat was **gone.**
Where could it have gone?

I looked in the garden.
I looked in the street.
I looked in the **bushes**.
But no hat.

I scratched my head
and looked up.
There was my hat!
It was in the tree!
I began to climb.

Then my hat began to move.
It jumped. It jiggled.
Two **baby** birds **popped** up over the brim.

"*Tweet*," they cried.
"*Tweet, tweet*."

My hat was now a **nest**.
If I took my hat back,
where would the birds live?
I went inside to think.

I came out later with lots
of old hats.
"Take any old hat you want,"
I told the birds.
"I just want my new hat back."

The birds took the old hats.
I climbed up the tree
to get my new hat.
The baby birds
were in a new old hat.
Everyone now had a hat
and a home.

★ What do the words in **dark print** mean? Other words
  in the story can help you. Draw a line under the words
  that help you. ★

WORD MEANINGS

Write the word for each meaning. Use the words in the box.

popped	gone	bushes
baby	nest	ground

1. small trees with many branches

_____

2. very young

_____

3. the land

_____

4. not there

_____

5. a home for birds

_____

6. moved fast

_____

Puzzle Fun

Solve the puzzle. Use the pictures, sentences, and words in the box.

popped	gone	bushes
baby	nest	ground

Across

1.

2. The toy _____ out of the box.

3.

Down

4. A puppy is a _____ dog.

5. I lost my book. It is _____.

6. We planted seeds in the _____.

GET WISE TO TESTS

Which word fits in the blank? Darken the circle for the correct answer.

 **Tip** Read carefully. Use the other words in the sentences to help you choose the correct word.

We wanted some small trees. My dad bought some ___(1)___. Then we dug a hole in the ___(2)___.

1. ○ flowers
  ○ water
  ○ bushes
  ○ pigs

2. ○ cloud
  ○ ground
  ○ house
  ○ green

I saw some birds in their ___(3)___. Then they flew away. Now they are ___(4)___. I cannot find them.

3. ○ room
  ○ noise
  ○ bus
  ○ nest

4. ○ gone
  ○ pretty
  ○ near
  ○ blue

My ___(5)___ brother is three years old. It was time to get up. He ___(6)___ out of bed.

5. ○ baby
  ○ dad
  ○ ball
  ○ girl

6. ○ dug
  ○ burned
  ○ listened
  ○ popped

Writing

Uncle Foster was a mouse. He shared his hats with birds. What other kind of animal might share? What could it share? Who could it share with? Write a story about the animal. Use some vocabulary words.

_____

_____

_____

_____

_____

_____

_____

_____

_____

Turn to "My Word List" on page 101. Write some words you would like to know more about. Choose words from the story or other words. Use a dictionary to find the meanings.

87

★ Read the story below. Think about the meanings of the words in **dark print**. ★

Sharing a Park

John Muir loved Yosemite Park.
He climbed the high **mountains**.
He walked in the forests of tall trees.
He **watched** the wild animals.
He saw things some people had
never seen.

Many people moved close to the park.
Some had sheep.
The sheep ate the grass in the park.
People cut down trees in the park, too.
They built houses with the wood.
Losing grass and trees was not good.
There was **trouble** in the park.

John Muir did not want the people
and sheep to hurt Yosemite.
He had a plan to **save** the park.

John Muir wrote letters to newspapers.
He **spoke** to people everywhere.
He told them about Yosemite.
Many people worked together to
save the park.

Thanks to John Muir, Yosemite was saved.
Many people now visit the pretty park.
People, plants, and animals share this
beautiful place.

★ What do the words in **dark print** mean? Other words
  in the story can help you. Draw a line under the words
  that help you. ★

SENTENCE CLUES

Read the sentences. Complete them with a word from the box.

mountains	**watched**	**trouble**
save	**spoke**	**beautiful**

1. Sam and Missy looked up at the sky. They

_____ the clouds.

2. We had _____

with our car. It would not start.

3. Sonja's hair looked very pretty. She had

a _____ bow in it.

4. We _____ to my aunt.

We told her about the party.

5. The fish is out of the water. We need to

_____ it.

6. Dad and I drove higher and higher into the

_____. We saw snow

on the tops of them.

WORDS WITH THE SAME MEANING

Read each sentence. Find the word in the box that means the same as the underlined word or words. Write the word on the line.

beautiful	watched
spoke	mountains

1. _____ David <u>talked</u> to his friends at school.

2. _____ Blanca <u>looked at</u> the TV in her mom's room.

3. _____ Mr. Han grows <u>pretty</u> flowers every spring.

4. _____ We flew in a plane over the <u>tall hills</u>.

ABC Order

The words in each row should be in ABC order. Write the missing word. Use the words in the box. The alphabet below can help you.

mountains	watched	trouble
save	beautiful	

1. present _____ travel

2. _____ careful drops

3. letter _____ named

4. teacher visit _____

5. spoke _____ vegetables

A B C D E F G H I J K L M N O P Q R S T U V W X Y Z

Which answer means the same as the underlined word? Darken the circle for the correct answer.

 **Tip** More than one answer may make sense. But only one has the same meaning as the underlined word.

1. <u>watched</u> the cars
   - ○ looked at
   - ○ sat on
   - ○ called to
   - ○ wished for

2. climbed <u>mountains</u>
   - ○ old trees
   - ○ big buildings
   - ○ tall hills
   - ○ my ladders

3. <u>save</u> the kitten
   - ○ keep from hurt
   - ○ feed today
   - ○ sleep with
   - ○ play with

4. <u>beautiful</u> flowers
   - ○ growing
   - ○ yellow
   - ○ new
   - ○ pretty

5. having <u>trouble</u>
   - ○ a truck
   - ○ a problem
   - ○ a plan
   - ○ a race

6. <u>spoke</u> on the phone
   - ○ hid
   - ○ heard
   - ○ talked
   - ○ fell

Writing

John Muir wrote letters about Yosemite. He wanted to save the park. Write a letter to a friend. Tell your friend about John Muir and Yosemite. Use some vocabulary words.

Dear _____,

_____

_____

_____

_____

_____

_____

_____

Your friend,

_____

Turn to "My Word List" on page 101. Write some words you would like to know more about. Choose words from the story or other words. Use a dictionary to find the meanings.

★ To review the words in Lessons 10–12, turn to page 98. ★

Read the words in the box. Then write the word that answers each riddle. Use the Dictionary if you need help.

| above | clean | oranges |
| flowers | soup | travel |

1. You can go from place to place.

   What can you do? _____

2. We are a plant part. We make seeds.

   What are we? _____

3. I am a food. I have other foods in me.

   What am I? _____

4. I am higher than something else.

   Where am I? _____

5. We are a kind of fruit. We are sweet.

   What are we? _____

6. I make my room neat.

   What do I do? _____

REVIEW

Read each question. Think about the meaning of the underlined word. Then write <u>yes</u> or <u>no</u> to answer the question. Use the Dictionary if you need help.

1. My dog <u>chased</u> me.

Did it run after me? _____

2. You see a <u>kitten</u>.

Is it a baby squirrel? _____

3. A baby <u>waved</u> to you.

Did it fly to you? _____

4. Marco got a <u>present</u>.

Did he get a gift? _____

5. Jenny is <u>hungry</u>.

Does she need food? _____

6. Ling planted <u>corn</u>.

Did she plant a tree? _____

Read the words in the box. Then write the word that answers each riddle. Use the Dictionary if you need help.

rings	missing	tale
trunk	forgot	candles

1. I am lost.

What am I? _____

2. You light us for special times.

What are we? _____

3. I am the main stem of a tree.

What am I? _____

4. You can tell me or read me.

What am I? _____

5. I did not remember.

What did I do? _____

6. We show the age of a tree.

What are we? _____

Read each question. Think about the meaning of the underlined word. Then write yes or no to answer the question. Use the Dictionary if you need help.

1. Chad has a tiny pet.

   Is it very big? _____

2. The bee is close to Ana.

   Is it near her? _____

3. You sat on the ground.

   Were you on the land? _____

4. The bird made a nest.

   Did it make a sign? _____

5. Jack had trouble with his truck.

   Did he have a problem with it? _____

6. You spoke to your teacher.

   Did you write a note to her? _____

REVIEW AND WRITE

The stories in this book have pictures to go with them. Choose your favorite story. Draw a new picture to go with it. Then tell what your picture shows. Use some vocabulary words you have learned.

_____

_____

_____

_____

My Word List

This is your word list. Here you can write words from the stories. You can also write other words that you would like to know more about. Use a dictionary to find the meaning of each word. Then write the meaning next to the word.

UNIT 1
FOOD FUN

UNIT 2
SPECIAL FRIENDS

MY WORD LIST

UNIT 3
COUNT ON IT

_____

_____

_____

_____

_____

UNIT 4
SHARING

_____

_____

_____

_____

_____

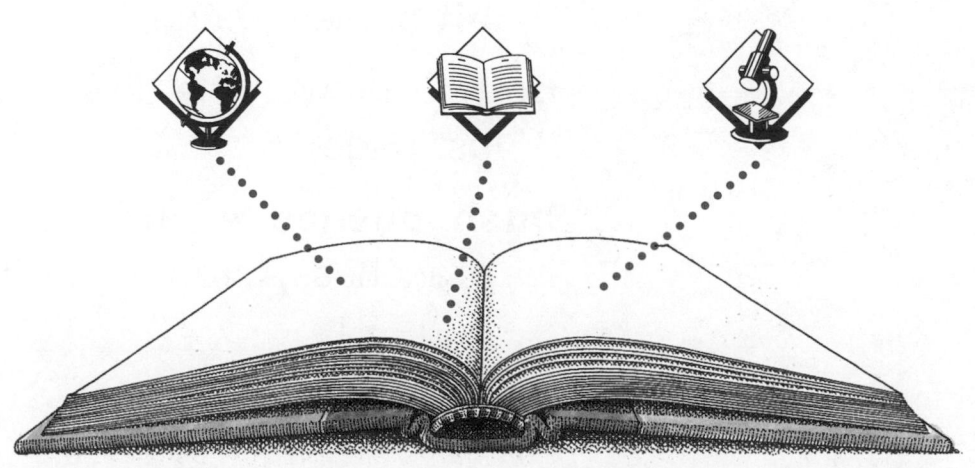

DICTIONARY

Aa

above Higher than. Planes fly **above** the clouds. page 7

age How old something is. Do you know the **age** of that boy? page 50

ago In the past. I started school two months **ago**. page 66

Bb

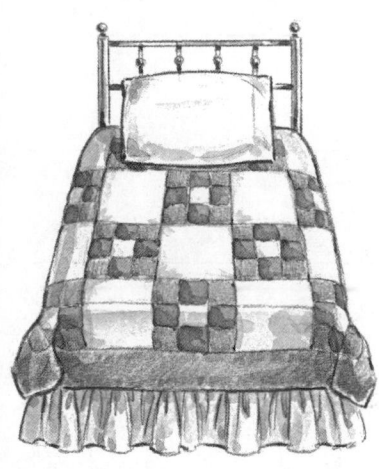

baby Very young. I have a **baby** brother. page 82

bark The outside cover of a tree. Many trees have brown **bark**. page 51

beautiful Pretty. The flowers are **beautiful**. page 89

best Better than all others. Ping is my **best** friend. page 35

bit, bits A little piece. My soup had only one **bit** of meat. page 75

both The two. The dog belongs to **both** of us. page 75

bush, bushes A small tree with many branches. A frog hopped under the **bush.** page 81

Cc

candle, candles A stick of wax that burns to give light. The **candle** gave off a yellow light. page 67

careful Gentle. You must be **careful** with the baby. page 29

catch, caught To get. I can **catch** the ball. page 56

chase, chased, chasing To run after. The dog **chased** the cat. page 29

clean To wash or make neat. We will **clean** our room. page 15

close Near. Tran lives **close** to the school. page 75

coat Something that covers. A cat has a **coat** of fur. page 74

corn A plant that people grow for food. We had **corn** for dinner. page 43

Dd

dish, dishes A thing that holds food. Ping put the apples in a **dish**. page 13

drop, drops To let fall. Do not **drop** food on the floor. page 75

Ee

eat, ate To take in food through the mouth. I **ate** an apple. page 14

explain, explains To make clear. Please **explain** why the sky is blue. page 67

Ff

family A group of related people. There are four boys in my **family**. page 66

first Before all others. Ed was **first** in line. page 43

flower, flowers The plant part that makes seeds. This **flower** smells very good. page 7

forget, forgot, forgetting To not remember. Did you **forget** your hat? page 59

Gg

gather To pick or get. We will **gather** the nuts in our yard. page 21

gone Not there. The cookies are **gone**. page 81

ground The land. We sat down on the **ground**. page 80

Hh

hope, hoped, hoping To wish for. I **hope** that snake is not real. page 66

hungry Needing food. I am very **hungry**. page 42

Ii

invite, invited, inviting To ask someone to do something. I will **invite** my friends to a party. page 43

Kk

kind Giving help. You should be **kind** to other people. page 42

kitten A baby cat. I watched the **kitten** play. page 28

Ll

leaf, leaves One of the flat, green parts of a plant. I picked a **leaf** from the tree. page 7

letter A written message. Ramon wrote a **letter** to his friend. page 34

Mm

missing Lost. My socks are **missing**. page 57

mountain, mountains A tall hill made of rocks. We could not climb to the top of the **mountain**. page 88

much A lot of. We did not get **much** snow this year. page 20

Nn

name, named, naming To give a name to. We will **name** the baby Sarah. page 28

nest A home for birds and some other kinds of animals. The bird's **nest** has an egg in it. page 82

notice, noticed, noticing To see. Did you **notice** that strange bug? page 50

Oo

orange, oranges A kind of fruit. I ate an **orange** at breakfast. page 20

Pp

pack, packed To put together. We will **pack** our old toys in boxes. page 21

party A time for fun. Nina is having a birthday **party**. page 34

pop, popped, popping To move fast. I will **pop** out of bed. page 82

present A gift. Burt will buy a **present** for his sister. page 37

Qq

quite Very. The ring was **quite** old. page 15

Rr

ring, rings A circle. The lion jumped through a **ring** of fire. page 50

root The plant part that grows in the dirt. A **root** helps a plant get water. page 6

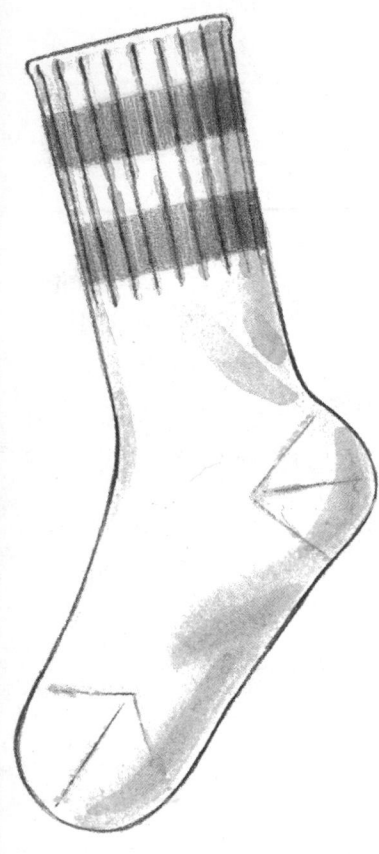

Ss

save, saved, saving To keep from being hurt. Help us **save** the sea turtles. page 89

shout, shouted To yell. We will **shout** for our team at the game. page 61

soup A food made with water and pieces of other foods. We put ham in the **soup**. page 12

speak, spoke To talk. Opal will **speak** with her friend. page 89

spring The time of year between winter and summer. Trees grow leaves in the **spring**. page 42

stir, stirred, stirring To mix with a spoon. I will **stir** the soup. page 12

store A place that sells things. We can buy some milk at the **store**. page 6

supper The last meal of the day. We will have ham for **supper**. page 57

Tt

tale A story. That **tale** is true. page 66

teacher A person who shows others how to do something. We have a new **teacher** for our class. page 28

tiny Very small. A ladybug is a **tiny** animal page 74

travel To go from one place to another. We will **travel** by bus. page 20

trouble A problem. William got in **trouble** when he was late. page 88

trunk The main stem of a tree. The squirrel built a nest in the **trunk** of the tree. page 50

Vv

vegetable, vegetables A kind of plant that we eat part of. Carrots are my favorite **vegetable.** page 6

visit To go to see. I went to **visit** my grandmother. page 28

Ww

watch, watched To look at. We like to **watch** airplanes fly. page 88

wave, waved, waving To move a hand to say hello or good-by. I will **wave** to my father. page 36

wood The inside part of a tree. This chair is made of **wood.** page 51

wonder To want to know. I **wonder** why Yuko is late. page 35

worker, workers A person doing work. That **worker** does her job well. page 21

wrong Not right. My dad drove up the **wrong** road. page 58

ANSWER KEY

UNIT 1 FOOD FUN

LESSON 1
Eat Your Vegetables!

WORD MEANINGS
1. leaves
2. above
3. flowers
4. store
5. root
6. vegetables

WORD GROUPS
1. above
2. root
3. vegetables
4. store

GET WISE TO TESTS
1. leaves
2. above
3. store
4. vegetables
5. root
6. flowers

WRITING
Answers will vary based on students' personal experiences.

LESSON 2
Lunch

WORD MEANINGS
1. clean
2. dishes
3. ate
4. stir
5. soup
6. quite

WORD GROUPS
1. clean
2. dishes
3. soup
4. stir

GET WISE TO TESTS
1. a food
2. wash
3. very
4. mix
5. took In food
6. plates

WRITING
Answers will vary based on students' personal experiences.

LESSON 3
From the Tree to You

SENTENCE CLUES
1. travel
2. oranges
3. packed
4. workers
5. much
6. gather

WORDS WITH THE SAME MEANING
1. filled
2. helpers
3. get

WORDS WITH OPPOSITE MEANINGS
1. stay
2. little

PUZZLE FUN

Across	Down
1. workers	4. oranges
2. gather	5. much
3. packed	6. travel

GET WISE TO TESTS
1. get
2. people doing work
3. a kind of fruit
4. go
5. a lot of
6. put together

WRITING
Answers will vary based on students' personal experiences.

UNIT 2 SPECIAL FRIENDS

LESSON 4
Koko's Friend

WORD MEANINGS
1. teacher
2. careful
3. named
4. kitten
5. chased
6. visit

ABC ORDER
1. above, careful, flowers
2. kitten, leaves, named
3. quite, travel, visit
4. teachers, vegetables, workers

GET WISE TO TESTS
1. ran after
2. person who teaches
3. baby cat
4. gentle
5. gave a name to
6. go to see

WRITING
Answers will vary based on students' personal experiences.

LESSON 5
The Surprise Party

WORD MEANINGS
1. letter
2. best
3. party
4. waved
5. wonder
6. present

PUZZLE FUN

Across	Down
1. best	4. letter
2. waved	5. party
3. present	6. wonder

GET WISE TO TESTS
1. want to know
2. message
3. gift
4. better than all others
5. moved his hand
6. time for fun

WRITING
Answers will vary based on students' personal experiences.

LESSON 6
Thankful for a Friend

SENTENCE CLUES
1. spring
2. corn
3. kind
4. first
5. invited
6. hungry

WORDS WITH OPPOSITE MEANINGS
1. spring
2. first
3. kind

WORD GROUPS
1. invited
2. corn
3. spring

ABC ORDER
1. first
2. spring
3. kind
4. invited
5. corn
6. hungry

GET WISE TO TESTS
1. invited
2. kind
3. hungry
4. first
5. spring
6. corn

WRITING
Answers will vary based on students' personal experiences.

UNIT 3 COUNT ON IT

LESSON 7
Birthdays for a Tree

WORD MEANINGS
1. trunk
2. notice
3. age
4. rings
5. bark
6. wood

WORDS WITH MORE THAN ONE MEANING
1. b   2. a   3. a

GET WISE TO TESTS
1. circles
2. how old something is
3. the inside of a tree
4. see
5. outside cover of a tree
6. main stem

WRITING
Answers will vary based on students' personal experiences.

LESSON 8
Five Silly Fishermen

WORD MEANINGS
1. missing
2. supper
3. forgot
4. shouted
5. wrong
6. catch

WORDS WITH OPPOSITE MEANINGS
1. shouted
2. forgot
3. wrong
4. missing
5. catch
6. supper

GET WISE TO TESTS
1. didn't remember
2. missing
3. shouted
4. not right
5. get
6. evening meal

WRITING
Answers will vary based on students' personal experiences.

LESSON 9
It's Time For Kwanzaa!

SENTENCE CLUES
1. candles
2. family
3. hope
4. tale
5. explains
6. ago

ABC ORDER
1. family, invited, kind
2. ago, bark, candles
3. shouted, tale, wood
4. explains, hope, invited

PUZZLE FUN

Across	Down
1. ago	4. family
2. explains	5. hope
3. tale	6. candles

GET WISE TO TESTS

1. tale	4. family
2. ago	5. hope
3. candles	6. explains

WRITING
Answers will vary based on students' personal experiences.

UNIT 4 SHARING

LESSON 10
Sharing Under the Sea
WORD MEANINGS

1. drops	4. bits
2. close	5. coat
3. tiny	6. both

WORD GROUPS

1. both	3. close
2. tiny	

WORDS WITH MORE THAN ONE MEANING
1. a   2. b

GET WISE TO TESTS

1. very little	4. lets fall
2. covering	5. the two
3. small pieces	6. near

WRITING
Answers will vary based on students' personal experiences.

LESSON 11
Uncle Foster's Garden Hat
WORD MEANINGS

1. bushes	4. gone
2. baby	5. nest
3. ground	6. popped

PUZZLE FUN

Across	Down
1. bushes	4. baby
2. popped	5. gone
3. nest	6. ground

GET WISE TO TESTS

1. bushes	4. gone
2. ground	5. baby
3. nest	6. popped

WRITING
Answers will vary based on students' personal experiences.

LESSON 12
Sharing a Park
SENTENCE CLUES

1. watched	4. spoke
2. trouble	5. save
3. beautiful	6. mountains

WORDS WITH THE SAME MEANING

1. spoke	3. beautiful
2. watched	4. mountains

ABC ORDER

1. save	4. watched
2. beautiful	5. trouble
3. mountains	

GET WISE TO TESTS

1. looked at	
2. tall hills	
3. keep from hurt	
4. pretty	
5. a problem	
6. talked	

WRITING
Answers will vary based on students' personal experiences.

UNIT 1 REVIEW

1. travel	4. above
2. flowers	5. oranges
3. soup	6. clean

UNIT 2 REVIEW

1. yes	4. yes
2. no	5. yes
3. no	6. no

UNIT 3 REVIEW

1. missing	4. tale
2. candles	5. forgot
3. trunk	6. rings

UNIT 4 REVIEW

1. no	4. no
2. yes	5. yes
3. yes	6. no

REVIEW AND WRITE
Answers will vary based on students' personal experiences.